What Readers and Critics say about the Poetry of Felix Dennis

'His poetry sings like a summer breeze
through the fairground.'
— Sir Paul McCartney, musician & songwriter

'He is the very essence of English poetry
— lyrical, rhythmic, emotional.'
— Jon Snow, television newscaster

'I love his poetry. With moments of
real genius, some of his poems will
last as long as poetry is read.'
— Benjamin Zephaniah, poet,
Sky Arts television documentary

'Felix Dennis is the real thing.
I love reading his verse and you will, too.'
— Stephen Fry, actor, writer & director

'The uncrowned Poet Laureate...
he writes in the language of the soul.'
— Christopher Rush, author

'If Waugh were alive, he would fall
on Dennis's verse with a glad cry
of recognition and approval.'
— John Walsh, *The Independent*

'I enjoy his poetry immensely.'
— Mick Jagger, singer & songwriter

'An engaging monster, filled with
contradictions and reeking of sulphur.'
— *The Times*

'He invokes sorrow as fast as regret,
pain as readily as passion, love as tenderly
as murderous rage.'
— Shirley Conran, OBE, author

'Irresistible and superb...
the best new poet of the 21st-century.'
— Tom Wolfe, critic & author,
Sky Arts television documentary

'The most satisfying collection
of poetry I have ever read.'
— Tracy Farnsworth, editor,
roundtablereviews.com

'Beautifully crafted, accessible
and unforgettable. To watch him
perform is pure magic.'
— Clare Fitzsimmons, *Stratford Observer*

'At least one of these poems will
be instantly anthologised.'
— Melvyn Bragg, broadcaster & author

'Total, utter joy... so real, so readable
and so enjoyable.'
— Richard Fair, *bbc.co.uk*

'Talent at once wise and maddeningly
childish, optimistic and grim.'
— Dawn French, actor and comedienne

'You feel he lived it so richly,
so dangerously to be so wise for our delight.'
— Dr. Robert Woof,
Director of *The Wordsworth Trust*

'He makes it look easy, damn him!
I couldn't put the book down.'
— Z. Menthos, *critic.org*

'...eloquently observant, beautifully
crafted poetry.'
— Hannah Gal, critic, *The Huffington Post*

'*Homeless In My Heart* is so brilliant I need to
keep one by me. He grabs you and pulls you
in from the first word. A master of his craft.'
— Mary Doe, reader, *amazon.co.uk*

'What he has done is make poetry accessible
to thousands, if not millions, of people.'
— Patricia McCarthy , editor, *Agenda*

This is The Way of The World

REAL LIFE POETRY

J3
9/14

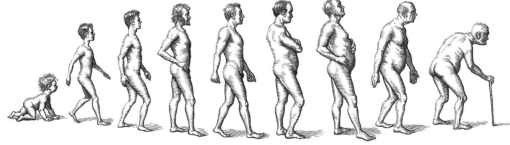

In poetry —
I am the one I could have been,
The one I would have been
       Had nurture not dispensed with art.

In poetry —
I am the one who jeered at fear,
Who whispered in its ear:
       Fool! Fight or flight is all one art.

In poetry —
I am the one I longed to be,
The sailor home from sea,
       This chart, this compass, all my art.

But life is
       not poetry.

This is The Way of The World

REAL LIFE POETRY

Felix Dennis

Illustrated by Bill Sanderson

Book and cover design by Rebecca Jezzard

EBURY
PRESS

1 3 5 7 9 10 8 6 4 2

Published in 2014 by Ebury Press, an imprint of Ebury Publishing

A Random House Group Company

The Random House Group Limited Reg. No. 954009

Addresses for companies within the Random House Group can be found at
www.randomhouse.co.uk

A CIP catalogue record for this book is available from the British Library

The Random House Group Limited supports the Forest Stewardship Council® (FSC®),
the leading international forest-certification organisation. Our books carrying the
FSC label are printed on FSC®-certified paper. FSC is the only forest-certification scheme
supported by the leading environmental organisations, including Greenpeace.
Our paper procurement policy can be found at **www.randomhouse.co.uk/environment**

To buy books by your favourite authors and register for offers
visit www.randomhouse.co.uk

Illustrator: Bill Sanderson
Designer: Rebecca Jezzard
Production: Caroline Rush

Set in Minion Pro and Ideal Sans

Printed and bound in the UK by Butler Tanner and Dennis Ltd.
Frome and London.

For my old school chums
and early bandmates,
especially

Stuart Baird
Ken Daughters
Roger Hillier
Martin Jones
John Leaver
Terry Murphy
Richard Ongley
Johnny Pell
Peter Quesnel
Bruce Sawford
David Teasdale
David Wallbank
Tony Woollcott
Richard Wyse

and the mums and dads
who tolerated and paid for us
and the club and the pub managers
who booked us
and the drivers and roadies
who humped for us
and those girlfriends
who put up with us
and all the musicians
who inspired us
and the engineers
who recorded us
and
the fans

Contents

A Note on the Poems

I began writing poetry, unexpectedly, in 1999 while recovering from an illness. I was then in my early fifties — pretty late as these things go. One newspaper journalist has observed that I write 'prolifically and like a man obsessed': perhaps, subconsciously — if indeed there is such a thing — I have been attempting to make up for all that lost time?

I attempt to write for at least a few hours a day on the basis of Mark Twain's dictum that for authors 'most inspiration comes from the application of the seat of the pants to the seat of the chair'. I constantly make notes, having discovered that if a promising line or subject arrives in my head, I must record it immediately. Delay is often fatal to its recovery.

For the first few years I found myself writing four or even five poems a week — a virtual cataract. This has now settled down somewhat. I calculate that in the past fourteen years I have spent 19,000 hours attempting to compose verse — close to a quarter of my waking life!

Sometimes I write poetry directly onto my computer. No difference is apparent (to me at least) in the quality of poems created on my computer compared with those begun on paper. When I'm done with a poem, I squirrel it away and try not to refer to it for a year or so. I revise only to make selections for a new book or poetry tour. I always attempt to keep in mind the observation of an earlier poet who wisely pointed out that no poem is ever really 'finished'; merely 'finished *with*' by its author.

Occasionally, I get stuck. Either I cannot write anything worthwhile or I suspect that the form or meter I am wrestling with has usurped the poem's original *raison d'être*. When this happens, I force myself to abandon the blighter and bang it in a folder marked 'Poems In Progress'. In the early days I tended to soldier on, which often led to second-rate work. Other writers have helped me to come to understand that structure is merely a vessel, not the wine, and that spoiled wine in a fancy decanter is vinegar by any other name. I have also learned that a bad poem, or one merely strong in the weak places, is still a bad poem, no matter what the cost of its birth pains.

Some poems arrive effortlessly, others are the result of months of graft. There appears to be (forgive the pun) no rhyme and no reason to it. Sometimes I find writing poetry truly exhausting, mentally, spiritually and physically. On other occasions, especially when I am convinced I have created something worthwhile, I am invigorated even after hours of work.

Audience reaction plays a part in the selection of poems for a new book. While no single audience is infallible, their collective view is nearly so, in my experience. Booze can help in writing, but only for an hour or so after the first glass of wine; later, mortifying gibberish is too often the result. Reading the work of other poets is inspirational, but dangerously beguiling. I love to read poetry, but I now separate that activity from my own verse-making.

What of intent? Do I write poetry to be performed, to be recorded, or to sit quietly on the page? As anyone familiar with the subject will confirm, some of our finest poets are, or were, poor readers of their own work. (To test this, visit the wonderful website created by Richard Carrington and Andrew Motion, **www.poetryarchive.org** which features, alongside much else, historical recordings by outstanding poets.) Even so, poetry is, in essence, an oral art, a form of song older by far than prose. Rhyme and meter developed partly as a mnemonic device — long before hieroglyphs were scratched onto rock or bark.

The answer, then, is that I write poetry to be read aloud while knowing that many of my readers will not do so; knowing, too, that only a small percentage will ever attend one of my public readings. Instead, my publishers include a free audio CD with all my poetry books. Having heard actors from the Royal Shakespeare Company read my poetry on stage, I'm aware that I have neither the talent nor training to match them. Even so, I sit in a studio three or four times a year recording my work. These recordings appear in the audio CDs found in my books, on my own website and others, on the special audio books created by libraries for the blind — and, when I'm lucky, on various radio and television programmes.

Does it all matter? Years ago a lady came up to me after a poetry reading. She was crying softly. As I signed her book, she said: 'How could you know? How could you know? You are not a mother. How could you know?'

She squeezed my shoulder as her husband led her into the night. So, yes. It bloody well *does* matter — to me and to her, at least.

While it is idle for authors to feign total indifference to applause or brickbats, all in all, I am convinced I write mainly for myself. One of America's most respected literary critics has called me 'the best poet writing in the English language.' At the same time, a respected London literary magazine has accused me of 'dragging English poetry single-handedly back to the Stone Age'. I try not to spend too much time gorging on 'the glories of triumph or failure' and keep on with the job, whether planting trees in my forest, encouraging young talent to make money (for me and for them) or creating the very best poetry I'm capable of.

I'm pretty sure I would continue to write verse if no one in the world expressed interest. I write to discover who I am, to escape the carapace inherited from a life in commerce, to stave off predilections for other addictions and, primarily, to experience the joy of weaving words to shape ideas and *vice versa*. As a somewhat noisome beast, perhaps I should have inflicted my verse-making onto the world anonymously, using a *nom de plume* — the very advice I received from well-meaning friends years ago — but to have done so would have deprived me of the pleasure of performing my work in public.

As Lord Chesterton remarked: 'It is hell to write but heaven to have written.' Amen to that, would say most writers. Why then do we continue to plumb the depths of Chesterton's hell? For some, like Dr. Johnson, the answer might be, 'to make a living': (not that I believe him for a minute). For others, 'to make a reputation' or simply, 'because I can'. For me, it is the result of a chance discovery made all those years ago in a hospital bed: that the flame of poetry cauterizes the wound of life as nothing else can.

Readers wishing to learn more, or to watch or listen to me performing my poetry, or to read my poems online, (published and unpublished), will find a warm welcome on my website at **www.felixdennis.com**

Mandalay, Mustique, St Vincent and the Grenadines, West Indies
January 2014

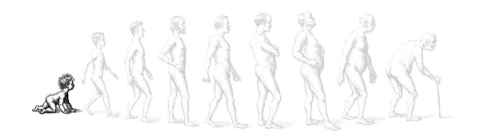

Infant

Song for a Child, Newly Born

May your thoughts be with the living,
    May your hand and eye be swift,
May your thanks be with the giving
    And never with the gift.

May your kindness be unfailing,
    May your ship glide by each shoal,
May the helmsman of each sailing
    Be the captain of your soul.

May you pass through all life's dangers,
    May your lovers all be true,
May you learn that this world's strangers
    Were friends you never knew.

May your laughter ring like fountains,
    May your heart be wild and free,
May you walk among the mountains
    But live beside the sea.

Mandalay, Mustique   December 26, 2004

The Road is Made by Walking

The road is made by walking,
    Abreast or single file.
While idlers sit there gawking, child,
    Come walk with me a while.

No miles are made by talking,
    No map can stride a mile.
The road is made by walking, child,
    Come walk with me a while.

Dorsington, Warwickshire April 12, 2005

"Wanderer, your footsteps are the road,
and nothing more;
wanderer, there is no road, the road
is made by walking."
    — Antonio Machado, (1875-1939)

Conversation with a Child
by 'The Cotton House' Pond

Why do they call them dragonflies?
The only answer is: we do —
The names of things are often lies.
But why do they call them dragonflies?
And are those diamonds in their eyes?
Why, bless you, child, I wish I knew.
So why do they call them dragonflies?
The only answer is: we do.

Mandalay, Mustique   April 14, 2006

Triolets are not exactly a popular verse form today — if, indeed, they ever were in English poetry.
W. H. Auden apparently thought them too trivial to bother with, and I would bow unhesitatingly to
his genius in such matters. But a triolet just sort of happened in the above lines — perhaps it suited the
repetitive nature of my young friend's questioning. And anyway, why <u>are</u> they called dragonflies?

Doll Talk

I know a girl called Jenny Bree
Who lives in Brighton-by-the-sea,
Her room is filled with dolls to hold —
Next year she will be six years old.

While Jenny dreams, her dolls discuss
Their secrets. Some make such a fuss!
'It's odd we never change,' one cries,
'While Jenny grows before our eyes.'

A rag doll clasped in Jenny's arm,
Whispers then in hushed alarm:
'You silly-billys, talk is cheap
But Jenny needs her beauty sleep,

So keep you voices down, for shame!'
A teddy bear without a name
Growls out: 'All very well for you,
But I have heard, and think it true,

That when young Jen grows up one day
Then we will all be thrown away
And chucked upon a rubbish dump.'
'Oh, Teddy, you are such a grump,'

Chirps Molly with the bright red hair,
'As if our Jen would leave us there!
When I was lost a week ago
She had her Mum search high and low

To find me or she'd *die*, she said —
(She'd stuffed me underneath the bed).
So much for all your nasty thoughts;
You bears are always out of sorts.'

A Barbie in a chiffon dress
Pipes up: 'I think I'd best confess
That once, I was her sister's joy,
But now there's not a single toy

In Susan's room, unless she still
Has Monty on the window sill.'
'Who's Monty?' asks a doll, wide-eyed.
'My bridegroom,' sniffs the Barbie bride.

On hearing this a certain gloom
Descends upon young Jenny's room,
Until a pony, soft and pink,
Neighs out: 'I'll tell you what I think:

I do not think that any toy
Belongs to any girl or boy
For very long. But that don't mean
They didn't love us, Josephine.

I think that some are kept by chance
And others...' here she steals a glance
At Josie, '...they are passed along
To younger ones. I could be wrong...'

The bedroom fills with angry cries
As Jenny turns and softly sighs,
And all the dolls sit still as mice.
The rag doll says: 'Here's my advice:

There's none of us who really knows
What might be true when Jenny grows,
Nor do we know who made us all
Or what's beyond the garden wall,

But if I have to soak up tears
From other little ones, my dears,
And if it turns out Pony's right —
Then what will be will be. Goodnight!'

Mandalay, Mustique May 11, 2003

A Child of Adam and Eve

There are no 'immigrant children',
Cluttering up our shores;
There's only a tyke on a beat-up bike,
Who wants to play with yours.

There are no 'urchin children',
Scavenging on the street;
There is only a mite in endless flight,
And never enough to eat.

There are no 'working children',
Dollar a week for pay,
There's only a boy who packed the toy
We bought for Billy today.

There are no 'feral children',
Born and raised in a squat;
There's only the shell of a child in hell
Who gives as good as she got.

There are no 'foreign children',
The world is grown too small;
There's only the choice, a kindly voice
Or the shaming of us all.

There are no 'orphan children',
Whatever we may believe;
There is only this — a hug and a kiss
For a child of Adam and Eve.

New York City August 29, 2001

The Sky Is In The Puddle

'The sky is in the puddle, mummy! See?
     And all the clouds are sailing upside-down!
The apple tree is staring *up* at me,
     And all its leaves have gone a muddy brown!'

'You're seeing a reflection — look, my love,
     If I lean here, I think that you'll see me.'
'The trees can see themselves from up above?'
     'The older that we get, the less we see.'

Dorsington, Warwickshire   July 11, 2009

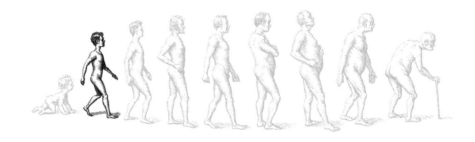

Schooldays

Enough

I wish you enough of a summer sun's measure
    To savour an apple tree's shade,
Enough of the mischief of youth and its pleasure
    For silence when others have strayed.

I wish you enough of the wisdom of learning
    To challenge the truths of the wise,
Enough of the road and a vagabond's yearning
    To wander and wear out your eyes.

I wish you enough of the madness of wooing
    As lusting and loving collide,
Enough of the blindness that shadows pursuing
    To bind you as passions subside.

I wish you enough of your getting and giving
    To fathom the value of both,
Enough of betrayal to grasp that forgiving
    Annuls any promise or oath.

I wish you enough of the kindness of others
    To temper the powers you wield,
Enough of the love of your sisters and brothers
    To barter your blade for a shield.

I wish you enough of the healing of laughter
    To bury each grief in its day,
Enough of forbearance, both here and hereafter,
    To wink at each dragon you slay.

I wish you enough of this life's Bacchanalia
    To swallow the sweet with the rough,
To gorge on the glories of triumph — and failure!
    Until your heart whispers: 'Enough!'

Dorsington, Warwickshire July 19, 2011

Reading For Fun

What could be better than reading a book in bed,
Lost in a wonderland, filling my teeming head
With people and places, stories that jostle in space,
Where pages are mirrors in which I glimpse a face
Who now and again peers out, while I peer back —
And I know it was me, before I'd learned the knack
Of reading for fun. So I wave my hand and smile:
"Hey! It's not so hard — let's read together a while!"

Mandalay, Mustique   August 18, 2013

Good With His Hands

Stacking the bonfire,
Laying the fuses,
Helping us light
The Catherine wheels and the rockets:
He was good with his hands —
When he took them out of his pockets.

Tweezing a splinter,
Sucking a bee-sting,
Heating a pin
To puncture a troublesome blister:
He was good with his hands —
When he kept them off of my sister.

Tiling the bathroom,
Fixing the boiler,
Coaxing a flame
From the pilot light in the Aga:
He was good with his hands —
When they weren't upending a lager.

Left like a rag doll,
Battered and sobbing,
Lying too still,
Curled up on the floor like a foetus:
He was good with his hands —
When he lurched through the door to beat us.

Dorsington, Warwickshire   October 30, 2005

School Sport

I never was much good at sport
Except cross-country in the wet,
We'd cut the course to keep it short
And end it with a cigarette.

We pitied those in leather pads
And whites, the kings of grass and dirt;
Who needs a bouncer in the nads
To stagger off — 'retired hurt'?

And as for rugger, snot and blood
Weren't in it — wallies! — theirs and ours,
Churning up the turf to mud
Converting ears to cauliflowers.

We didn't need no referee
For soccer — that were best of all;
When Billy took a penalty
God help the goalie by the wall.

The hockey girls, all squeals and grunts,
We'd watch to catch a flash of bum,
I scored in their pavilion once —
But that's another story, chum!

Dorsington, Warwickshire February 17, 2002

School Outing in a Deserted Hamlet

We stand within an instance of the future
Dry-salvaging the past — note how the moss
Has colonised the crannied bricks and doorframes,
The cankered oak beams twenty feet across;
How grass and bramble pull to their embraces
The shattered tiles and mortar from the floor,
How martins now are nesting in the rafters,
And there, a rusty key still in a door
That once, perhaps, kept children from a pantry,
From bottled jam and cider on the blocks...
Take care! the nettles there conceal old bedsprings,
The cellar now is home to Mrs. Fox.

Wood is strong — but time is stronger,
Bricks and mortar sink to clay;
Iron lives long — but rust lives longer,
Wind and rain sweep all away.

And here, I think, we'll find... the doorstep scraper...
Yes, here, you see, among these bindweed roots,
God help the sons and fathers in a hurry
Who failed to scrape the mud from off their boots!
And here a Belfast sink, now full of spiders
And droppings from a family of mice;
That crumbling work of art was once a mangle,
The cupboard in the corner held the spice.
I shouldn't risk the stairs — the joists are rotten,
The bedrooms house a colony of bats,
The handle here pumped water from the well-head,
These pegs held Sunday bonnets and best hats.

Wood is strong — but time is stronger,
Bricks and mortar sink to clay;
Iron lives long — but rust lives longer,
Wind and rain sweep all away.

All gone: the whitewashed fence, the byre, the orchard,
The privy, roofless now and soon to fall,
The garden choked with weeds, (save one survivor —
That damask rose you see upon the wall);
All gone, young friends; the wind and rain conspire
To grind away hard centuries of toil,
The beetling years, bedecked with rust and mildew,
Are mindless Goths, in league with famished soil.
We stand within an instance of the future,
Barbarians and levellers at the gate...
You laugh! but mould has little sense of humour:
Earth loves us little — if she knows no hate.

Wood is strong — but time is stronger,
Bricks and mortar sink to clay;
Iron lives long — but rust lives longer,
Wind and rain sweep all away.

Mandalay, Mustique   July 17, 2003

Someday

'Someday, I'll be as happy as you, you'll see,'
The cry of every child pressed to the glass
Peering in and wishing furiously
That he was peering out. 'You'll kiss my arse
One day, you'll see!' Then turning fast he runs
To cross the tracks, his face not wet with rain,
But wet enough; a boy who'll father sons
Who in their turn will curse and hoard their pain —
And mould it into vicious appetites
Wrapped up in hearts of saturated fat.
Then, like a dog gone suddenly mad that bites
His master's cruel hand, they'll eat the cat.
    Which cat is that? The one that has the cream,
    As you'll discover someday... while you scream.

Dorsington, Warwickshire August 27, 2012

The first line is taken from a comment from Charles 'Hank' Bukowski ('Buke, rhymes with 'puke', to his friends) as reported by Barry Miles in his eponymous biography of Bukowski published by Virgin Books. Bukowski was an American writer and poet — about whom the more said the better. Following an appalling childhood, he became a drunk for decades on end, spending much of his life whoring, feuding and considering which form of suicide might cause the most mayhem to those left behind... yet his writing redeemed him. Even *The New York Times* in their toffee-nosed, schoolmasterly review of Miles's book was forced to admit that the poet's work was: 'brutal, profane but darkly hilarious' although hastily reminding their readers that Bukowski's life was 'repellently debauched'. Well, of course it was. How else could he have written what he did?

The 'D' Word

I knew no father — nor much cared
    For those (it seemed to me)
Who filled the homes of other boys
    With wrath and tyranny.

I learned (and soon!) to stop my mouth:
    'My mother is divorced...'
Brought disapproving, sheepish smiles,
    And every smile was forced.

Still (true enough) with friends and peers,
    It set me worlds apart;
That 'D' word cleared a tiger's path —
    And broke my mother's heart.

Mandalay, Mustique July 27, 2004

Impossible to imagine now, but in the grammar school I attended in the late 1950s and early 1960s, out of 500 boys, only one that I knew of, aside from me, had divorced parents. I wonder what the percentage would be today — and whether, or not, we should care?

The Awkward Squad

If he told us once, by God,
    He must have told us twenty:
A dozen for the Awkward Squad!
    Christ! he gave us plenty...

This is for dumb insolence!
    And this is for your fooling!
Have you not a jot of sense?
    Early Sixties schooling...

Masters in their phony bates,
    Faces flush from drinking;
Prefects with their toady mates,
    Prodding, pointing, winking...

Rugby bullies in the scrum
    Measuring their willies;
New boys bawling for their mum,
    Hectors and Achilles...

Cane and ruler, chalk and book,
    Snot and spittle flying;
A deathly hush, the filthy look:
    'This boy isn't trying...'

If he told us once, by God,
    He must have told us twenty:
A dozen for the Awkward Squad!
    Christ! he gave us plenty...

Mandalay, Mustique   December 30, 2002

Masters and prefects performed acts of cruelty disguised as discipline in my schools that, today, would land them straight in court. I once saw a boy knocked senseless at his desk from a chemistry master's unexpected blow to the back of his head. I watched one gym teacher beat youngsters on their arse many a time with a plimsoll while they were straddled across a vaulting horse. If they pissed themselves they were forced to clean up the mess in front of their classmates. I witnessed a suave headmaster call boys out in front of a hushed assembly and force them to wait for an hour outside his study door so that those passing would know they were in for 'an interview with Mr. Bamboo', as he called it. Today, the pendulum has swung so far back that teachers are virtually unable to discipline pupils at all. Thus are the sins of the fathers visited upon successive generations.

The Ballad of 'Abdul' Rowe

I tell of a teacher, Abdul Rowe,
Who taught — not so many years ago —
In Northwood Hills, at a grammar school,
Where he changed the life of a callow fool.

> Thank you, Abdul, thank you!
> You looked a proper tyro —
> We thought you weird
> With your big black beard
> And a multi-purpose biro.

It was back in nineteen sixty-three,
And I was the king of form 4C,
A viper's tongue and last in class,
Lord, how the prefects whacked my arse!

> Thank you, Abdul, thank you!
> We may have been unruly,
> And pinned a note
> On the back of your coat,
> I apologise, Abdul, truly.

In those days I was a mouthy lout
With precious little to mouth about,
I kept the bullies off my back
By feeding masters cheek and flack.

> Thank you, Abdul, thank you!
> Forgive that little tartar
> Who brought you fame,
> A sly nickname,
> And turned you into a martyr.

Now Abdul Rowe was a substitute
On English Lit', a new recruit,
A softy, wet behind the ears —
(I knew we'd soon have him in tears).

> Thank you, Abdul thank you!
> You didn't rant or rave, sir.
> You didn't shout
> Or bang us about
> To force us to behave, sir.

He dressed far worse than any boy,
His suits were shabby corduroy,
He couldn't discipline a fly
(And he knew it, too, so he didn't try).

> Thank you, Abdul, thank you!   .
> We howled like drunk carousers,
> (Yes, it was me
> And Johnny P
> Who superglued your trousers.)

Through all this riot that poor saint
Would smile and never make complaint,
Until one day, out loud, he made
Us read *The Charge of the Light Brigade*.

> Thank you, Abdul, thank you!
> He read like a transformed giant!
> He struck 4C's
> Artillery,
> And the class became compliant.

He knew he'd hooked us then, by God!
And sure enough he cast a rod
Across that lake of clueless proles,
And reeled in a few stray souls.

> Thank you, Abdul, thank you!
> You won't recall those scholars.
> You never knew —
> But it was you
> Who made me a million dollars!

Envoi: Thank you, Abdul, thank you!
> By God, I wish you well, sir,
> And as you'll note
> From what I've wrote,
> I've half-way learned to spell, sir!

Soho, London   December 2 , 2000

There really was an 'Abdul' Rowe (whose first name I never did learn) at St. Nicholas Grammar School at Northwood Hills, Middlesex, in the early 1960's. And he really did change my life, although neither of us could have known it at the time. He once wrote in my exercise book beside an essay: "If you keep this up, Dennis, we'll have you in a Penguin paperback yet!". Forty years later, I still remember those words. The carrot is mightier than the stick! It was Mr. Rowe who taught me that poetry can be fun, can move you to tears, can help bind up the wounds of life in a way almost nothing else can.

The Elephant in the Room

The elephant in the room that isn't there —
He's hard to walk around. He's big and grey.
My Mummy says it's not polite to stare.

He never moves. He can't fit in a chair,
Just standing there. He's always in the way,
The elephant in the room that isn't there.

Sometimes, at night, I send a little prayer
For God to shoo him out so I can play.
My Mummy says it's not polite to stare

And if I do, she ruffles up my hair
And asks me what I learned in school today.
The elephant in the room that isn't there

Has squashed us all apart. It isn't fair,
But if I ask about him what they say
Is: 'Mummy says it's not polite to stare.'

The grown-ups are pretending not to care —
We never ask how long he wants to stay.
Dear elephant in the room who isn't there,
My Mummy says it's not polite to stare.

Mandalay, Mustique January 7, 2004

This is a reworking of a piece (author unknown) of the same name which has floated around the internet for years. It has been used in messages of bereavement, in political debates, in newspaper cartoons and goodness knows where else. The first section of the original reads:

There's an elephant in the room.
It is large and squatting, so it is hard to get around it.
Yet we squeeze by with "How are you?" and "I'm fine," and a thousand other
forms of trivial chatter. We talk about the weather. We talk about work.
We talk about everything else, except the elephant in the room.

Today, an elephant in the room is used as an everyday simile or metaphor for something that is affecting everyone involved but that nobody wants to talk about — so they just pretend it's not there. My version above is in the form of a villanelle — which is which is a very old French form of poetry from Medieval times with many odd repetitions.

The Tyre Swing

"This is a secret place."
Nor will the coming years erase
Its shadow-haunted trees beside the pools.
"There's just the three of us in the village now
And only we can slither through the thorn.
Grown-ups would need machines or tools
To get here. And why would they come, anyhow?
It took us days to drag the tractor tyre
Beneath the undergrowth and lash the rope
Around a branch with wire.
        We use the slope
To launch ourselves high up into the air.
A kingfisher sits on our tyre — I've drawn
A picture of him."
        None will ever share
The secret of the tyre swing, rotting there...
"This is a secret place."

Dorsington, Warwickshire October 1, 2010

30

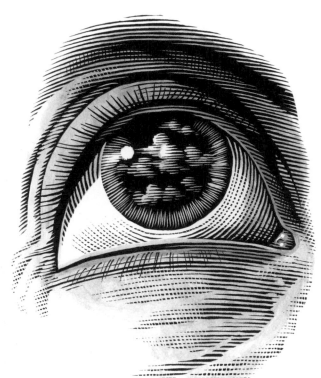

To Look And *See*

I like to look at things, to look and *see* —
The pattern left by brushes buffing suede;
Blonde eyelashes on pigs; the history
Of furniture that wax and use have made;

The mirror of the sky's strange alchemy
As clouds breed crawling colonies of shade;
A film of pollen dusted on a bee;
White mould within old jars of marmalade;

The hues of peeling bark upon a tree;
The knowing eyes of statues long decayed;
The sickly sheen of oil upon the sea;
The arc of craftsmen scribing with a blade;

Let's hang dull Habit's blindfold on its hook
And look and look to *see* — not just to look.

Dorsington, Warwickshire May 15, 2011

Johnny

Mummy! Johnny set my hair alight!
Mummy! Johnny super-glued the cat!
Mummy! Johnny got into a fight!
　　　(*And* he told the teacher she was fat).

Mummy! Johnny covered me in paint!
Mummy! Johnny farted for a bet!
Mummy! Johnny taught us how to faint!
　　　(*And* he let me share a cigarette).

Mummy! Johnny fell into the pool!
Mummy! Johnny taught me how to float!
Mummy! Johnny got expelled from school!
　　　(*And* he keeps a ferret in his coat).

Mummy! Johnny bought a new guitar!
Mummy! Johnny's gone and dyed his hair!
Mummy! Johnny kissed me in his car!
　　　(*And* I let him do it Mum, so there!)

Mandalay, Mustique　February 3, 2002

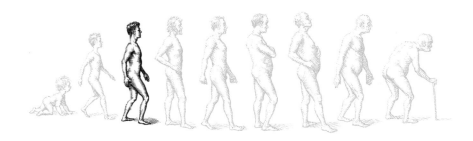

Adolescent

Advice To Any Daughter

Dearest, men are fools and know it.
Do not blame them overmuch —
Nor is it thought kind to show it
When it comes to love and such.

Bite your tongue and hide your laughter,
Though you read them like a book;
There is but one thing they're after
(Til they need a nurse or cook).

Charming, yes, but helpless babies,
Never buy one on a whim;
Test it first for lice or rabies —
Only then 'give in' to him.

Dearest, men are fools and know it.
One last thing before you go:
Make exception for a poet —
They, at least, know what *you* know!

Dorsington, Warwickshire April 8, 2003

Stretch McGuire

"Instinct," he said, "is a perilous thing,"
Then stuck his lower lip out like a tongue;
"Like a song you've heard but have never sung,
If you follow me. Why, I've seen men fling
Their lives away — and all because they cling
Like fools upon a ladder's rotten rung.
Or worse," he hawked and spat, "I've seen 'em hung
For following some ass who would be king."

Beneath the trees, crouched round a birch wood fire,
We sat as still as voles who sense a stoat,
Hoping that he'd go on. He cleared his throat
Again, tossing two branches on the pyre.
 "I knew a man, back when, called Stretch McGuire,
As clever as a whip — I've heard him quote
Whole passages from Shakespeare, learned by rote.
We called him Stretch for being such a liar.

At any rate, I served with him in France
In '44, 'cross Normandy, the Rhine —
By Christ! that bastard had a nose for wine —
Many's the time we slipped from the advance
And led the whole platoon a merry dance
While Stretch — who called the Sarge a Philistine
For drinking beer — would sneak troops from the line
To raid some chateau's cellar 'quite by chance'.

Six crates of Cheval Blanc to officers
And all would be forgiven, yet again!
Mind you, the brass were sots, hard-drinking men
And mostly useless with it, too, the curs.
One time, we dossed with Free-French saboteurs
And while we sat there, stripping down the Bren,
Stretch did a deal with 'em, right there and then,
To lead us to a place called Mille de Fleurs.

'They say the cellars there are bloody packed.'
'I'll bet you Jerry's cleared it out,' says I;
'I don't much like the look in this lot's eye.'
'No, no — they're sure the house is still intact —
Hand me the map.' The Frenchies jawed and quacked
And helped him trace the route we'd have to try.
We set off all together, by-and-by.
I wish I'd never gone. And that's a fact.

He were so sure. All doubt was a pariah:
'I feel it in my bones.' My arse! He led
Us straight into a trap. We turned and fled.
The Krauts had two score men behind barbed wire.
Six mates, including Stretch, died under fire.
Instinct is a perilous thing," he said.
"Christ, look at the time... you cut off home to bed —
Forget you ever heard of Stretch McGuire."

Mandalay, Mustique December 27, 2011

Ballad of the Treble Balls

(Harrow-on-the-Hill, 1965)

When once I found a wedding ring,
    (Whose ring it was I thought I knew),
I picked it up and pawned the thing
    To fetch myself a pound or two.

That night my conscience ups and stirs
    To set his hounds upon the track:
'You bloody fool, you know its hers,
    Now go and buy the damn thing back!'

I knew I'd crossed the line to thief,
    (*'I thought I knew'* was just a sop);
Dawn found me, suit in hand, beneath
    The treble balls of Satan's shop,

Though truth to tell, the demon there
    Was Solomon himself to me,
He weighed me with a knowing stare,
    His eyes as cold as charity —

For all the suit was poorly pressed,
    He swapped it for the ring, and then
He yawned: 'My son, I think it best
    I never see your face again.'

I took the ring and climbed the Hill
    To find its owner — gone away..!.
No forwarding address; worse still,
    They'd left a scribbled note to say:

'We've split for Goa. Tally-ho!
    & thanks for all the laughs, old mate,
We couldn't take the budgie, though,
    He's yours to keep, love Bill & Kate.'

Today my suits are custom built,
    They hang like convicts on parade
Beneath the treble balls of guilt —
    A debt of youth still yet unpaid.

Candlewood Lake, Connecticut February 16, 2003

This is a true story. The reference to Solomon is to a king of Israel 3,000 years ago, the son of David and Bathseba. Solomon was noted for his wisdom and justice. He is also presumed to be the author of the sensuous Song of Solomon in the Bible, though how he found time to write it with 1,000 wives and concubines is difficult to imagine!

Breasts

Some of the best are unexpected.
Fuller than one might have guessed,
Bouncing like puppies when released —
Innocence itself when dressed.

Others are conical dunces' caps,
Pink-tipped, self-supporting spears
Poorly sheathed by bras and blouses,
Yearning to be perfect spheres.

Melons are an embarrassment,
At least for now, but that will change!
As will the gamine's gentle curves
That time, too soon, will rearrange.

All flesh is false — and transitory,
Ripeness heralds its decay,
And yet your mottled, ebb-tide paps
Buoy me in their brown-ringed sway.

Candlewood, CT   August 31, 2010

Hippy Chick

(1950? - 1976)

Her face was painted white with gold mascara,
Her snake-hipped skirt no wider than a tie,
She wore a black beret, like Che Guevara,
And thigh-high velvet boots to make you cry.

Her nipples peek-a-booed through taut macramé,
Her junkie eyes were blanker than a mist,
Their hooded lids were gilded origami;
Her bangles jingle-jangled on her wrist.

Men hunted her as weasels hunt a rabbit,
I never heard a single word she said,
Nor cared about her hopes, her wants, her habit —
I would have died to take her once to bed.

They found her, comatose, in Ladbroke Garden,
By then she earned a living turning tricks.
It's damn all use — but still, I beg her pardon:
Young men are little more than walking dicks.

Mandalay, Mustique   July 5, 2003

The Jive Competition

Eastcote Youth Club, Middlesex, 1963

This was the night we'd been practising for,
But when she arrived at the hall she hissed:
'I hear you've been snogging that slut Maureen,
No use denying it, You were seen...'
And dug her fingernails into my wrist.
Then our names were called and we hit the floor.

She was cross, so cross she could barely speak,
Though oddly, both of us danced the better,
Her limbs like octopi, fuelled by rage...
And we won. But after we'd left the stage
She slapped me hard while I stood and let her —
I knew we'd be back in the sack next week.

Mandalay, Mustique   December 31, 2011

As the screenwriter Steve Ambrose put it: 'God created man with a penis and a brain, but only gave him enough blood to work one at a time.' And hey! I was only 15 years old. A name has been changed in this poem to protect the innocent. 'Jiving' was a popular rock'n'roll dance form in the 1950s and early 1960s involving strenuous physical effort and close cooperation between partners. Constant rehearsal was essential at competition level. The dance itself, which occasionally required the man to swing a girl literally between his legs and spin her like an unravelling top, encouraged a degree of physical intimacy which often led to its own consequences off the dance floor.

The House that Crack Built

This is the house that crack built.

This is the pipe
That lay in the house that crack built.

This is the puff,
That filled the pipe
That lay in the house that crack built.

This is the stuff,
That would not puff,
That filled the pipe
That lay in the house that crack built.

This is the sod,
That sold the stuff,
That would not puff,
That filled the pipe
That lay in the house that crack built.

This is the gun with the barrel sawn,
That shot the sod,
That sold the stuff,
That would not puff,
That filled the pipe
That lay in the house that crack built.

This is the room with the curtains drawn
That hid the gun with the barrel sawn,
That shot the sod,
That sold the stuff,
That would not puff,
That filled the pipe
That lay in the house that crack built.

This is the man who slept at dawn,
That lived in the room with the curtains drawn,
That sold the gun with the barrel sawn,

That shot the sod,
That sold the stuff,
That would not puff,
That filled the pipe
That lay in the house that crack built.

This is the frock all tattered and torn,
That kept the man who slept at dawn,
That lived in the room with the curtains drawn,
That sold the gun with the barrel sawn,
That shot the sod,
That sold the stuff,
That would not puff,
That filled the pipe
That lay in the house that crack built.

This is the maiden all forlorn,
That wore the frock all tattered and torn,
That kept the man who slept at dawn,
That lived in the room with the curtains drawn,
That sold the gun with the barrel sawn,
That shot the sod,
That sold the stuff,
That would not puff,
That filled the pipe
That lay in the house that crack built.

This is the babe that never was born,
That died in the womb of a maid forlorn,
That wore the frock all tattered and torn,
That kept the man who slept at dawn,
That lived in the room with the curtains drawn,
That sold the gun with the barrel sawn,
That shot the sod,
That sold the stuff,
That would not puff,
That filled the pipe
That lay in the house that crack built.

Mandalay, Mustique August 16, 2001

I know only too well of what I speak in this poem. My advice to anyone about to try crack is as follows: firstly, it will cost you more than you can pay — probably more than you can ever earn legally. Secondly, It will play havoc with your health in a very short time. Thirdly, because your personality will change, most of your friends will disown you — just as you will lose interest in anyone not taking or selling crack. Fourthly, you will almost certainly become addicted (and super-paranoid) very quickly indeed. Lastly, unless you quit early (difficult) and permanently (very, very difficult) the lifestyle and the drug itself will conspire to kill you. Apart from all that, it's great!

Anti-Social Behaviour Orders
(To the tune of Twinkle, Twinkle Little Star)

ASBO, ASBO, little law,
How we wonder what you're for,
Chavs and yobs who love to fight
Terrorise us every night.
Toothless, useless, little law,
How we wonder what you're for.

On the streets with hoods and knives,
How they terrorise our lives,
Though they all should be in bed,
All you do is boost their cred'.
ASBO, ASBO, can't you see
You are an accessory.

ASBO, ASBO, little law,
How we wonder what you're for,
Words will never rule the street,
We need coppers on the beat.
Toothless, useless, little law,
How we wonder what you're for.

Dorsington, Warwickshire   June 30, 2005

The Pity Of It All

'Who is the man who shouts so loud?' said Danny to his Dad.
'A Minister of State, I think. Now change the channel, son.'
'What's that he's shouting to the crowd?' said Danny to his Dad.
'It's mostly lies, 'his Dad replied. 'Now change the channel, son.
　　They must hold a new election, so they're swallowing their pride
　　While they're promising the earth to silly sods they can't abide,
　　But they'll sell us down the river, son, whatever we decide,
　　And the pity of it all — is that we let them.'

'Why do the ladies shake their fists?' said Lucy to her Mum.
'Them's lost their sons,' her Mum replied. 'Now change the channel, girl.'
'It says they fought the terrorists,' said Lucy to her Mum.
'That's what it says, but who was which? Now change the channel, girl.
　　When a soldiers gets 'is orders he must pack 'is kit and go,
　　Though I don't recall Afghanis ever bombing us in Bow,
　　And why the Queen don't send 'em back to barracks, I dunno,'
　　And the pity of it all — is that we lets 'em.'

'Who is the chap with checkered eyes?' said Danny to his Dad.
'That's Scotland Yard's Commissioner. Now change the channel, son.'
'And why should he apologise?' said Danny to his Dad.
'He's taking flak,' his Dad replied. 'Now change the channel, son.
    He's been busy chasing paperwork instead of chasing thieves,
    While his bosses set him targets not one officer believes,
    And he does it for the peerage they award him when he leaves,
    And the pity of it all — is that we let them.'

'Why do the children live in tents?' said Lucy to her Mum.
'They got no homes,' her mother said. 'Now change the channel, girl.'
'Why don't they build some? Makes no sense,' said Lucy to her Mum.
'They got no money, nor no food. Now change the channel, girl.
    They been slung out of their country though I couldn't tell you why,
    They say some of it's religion, but it's wickedness, says I,
    And the charities keeps feeding 'em, but still the kiddies die,
    And the pity of it all — is that we lets 'em.'

Mandalay, Mustique April 14, 2010

In her wonderful book 'Catching Life By The Throat: How To Read Poetry And Why', the author Josephine Hart, describes Rudyard Kipling's poem, 'Danny Deever' as 'a masterpiece of poetic, rhythmic perfection'. She backs up her claim with a quote from T. S. Eliot about 'Danny Deever': 'In the end, it is the pity that lingers.' Yes it is. But that quote of Eliot's lingered, too, while the drumbeat of Kipling's masterpiece echoed in my head, until I rose from my bed and did what no poet should do in earnest, for a pastiche is not a pretty thing, however fervently felt. Even so, the above is my tribute to a great English poet and to what is perhaps his best poem.

The Way Of The World

When backs are oak and girls are willing,
This is the way of the world,
When boasts are brave and beer's for swilling,
This is the way of the world.
  This is the way of the world, lad — aye!
  Travel and saddle and gun —
  The Devil to pay, a foreign sky,
  Kiss 'em and run,
  Chasing the sun,
  This is the way of the world.

When necks are swans and flesh is flawless,
This is the way of the world,
When waists are slim and boys are lawless,
This is the way of the world.
  This is the way of the world, lass — aye!
  Aching and faking and fears,
  A heart that leaps at a lover's cry,
  Glamour and tears,
  Galloping years,
  This is the way of the world.

When dreams are dying and and sinews soften,
This is the way of the world,
When sex is grand, but not as often,
This is the way of the world.
>   *This is the way of the world, now — aye!*
>   *Muddling and middling and blown,*
>   *The house too big and the bills too high,*
>   *The children flown,*
>   *Back on your own,*
>   *This is the way of the world.*

When eyes are clouds and teeth grow rotten,
This is the way of the world,
Mourning for what is already forgotten,
This is the way of the world.
>   *This is the way of the world, friend — aye!*
>   *Scraggy and baggy and thin,*
>   *Shedding the cloak with an easy sigh,*
>   *Naked as sin,*
>   *As you came in,*
>   *This is the way of the world!*

Dorsington, Warwickshire April 22, 2011

Useless Bastards

Me mum taught me to fight. She loved a knife
But I prefer an iron bar or boot.
I only ever lost once in me life:
I never thought that tooled-up sod would shoot —
The useless bastard.

We rule round here — the plods are effin' crap.
The only problem is CCTV.
But all you need's a scarf or baseball cap.
I duff 'em up — then take their wallet, see?
The useless bastards.

If you get nicked, stay shtoom and shut yer face.
It's self-defence — a plant — a poxy trance.
Then pray to get old Griffiths try yer case —
He's always good to hand out 'one last chance'.
The useless bastard.

Dorsington, Warwickshire June 9, 2009

Hacker-boy, hacker-boy
(To the tune of Pussycat, Pussycat, Where Have You Been?)

Hacker-boy, hacker-boy, where have you been?
   I sat in my bedroom and stared at a screen.
Hacker-boy, hacker-boy, what did you see?
   I built a new virus upon my PC.

Hacker-boy, hacker-boy, where is it now?
   It is shutting the lights off in Rome and Macao.
Hacker-boy, hacker-boy, what did you do?
   I proved that I'm better than anyone knew.

Hacker-boy, hacker boy, why do you smile?
   My virus has wormed through a Pentagon file.
Hacker-boy, hacker-boy, why are you sad?
   They put me in prison for being so bad.

Dorsington, Warwickshire May 30, 2004

To A God Child

Ask me for some money, dearest. Ask me for a loan.
Ask me why your parents' hearts are made of bloody stone.
Ask me for a stack of condoms. Ask me why I smoke.
Ask me why Bob Dylan mumbles: 'Life is but a joke...'
    Ask me out to dinner,
        You slothful little sinner;
            Introduce your newest lover,
                (I won't tell your bloody mother!)
You may ask me anything and never count the price...
Just, please, never ever dearest, ask me for advice.

Tell me if you're happy, dearest. Tell me if you're not.
Tell me you've a new tattoo and show me what you got.
Tell me you're in trouble and I'll walk with you to hell.
Tell me you are gay or bi (who else you gonna tell?)
    Tell me that you kissed her
        Or he kissed your stupid sister;
            Tell me you've been caught and bailed,
              Tell me the abortion failed;
You may tell me anything of pain or paradise...
Just, please, never ever dearest, offer *me* advice.

Mandalay, Mustique January 17, 2001

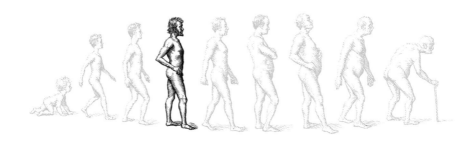

Lover

There May Come A Day

There may come a day when you will call
    And I do not reply,
When seas run dry, when mountains split and fall,
When hell-spawned horsemen occupy the sky
    And all returns to clay.
That day may come, my love —
            But not this day.

There may come a day when you will reach
    And I do not reach back,
My limbs too slack to remedy the breach,
My mind grown mutinous — too dull to track
    The order to obey.
That day may come, my love —
            But not this day.

There may come a day when love shall fail,
    When we shall cease to care,
When what we share blooms colourless and stale
And scarlet passions fade beyond repair
    To sickly shades of grey.
That day may come, my love —
            But not this day!

Mandalay, Mustique August 19, 2009

A Flawed Rose

What perfect Juliet or Mr. Right
Ever drew breath? Trust me in this, my dear.
No sooner do such paragons appear
And sweep us from our eager feet one night
To realms of shuddering bliss and stunned delight,
Than imperfections creep upon the ear
Or eye. Even as longing draws us near,
Some blemish brings them tumbling from their height.
Nor can we leaven heartbreak with surprise:
Who was it placed them on a pedestal,
These idols unalloyed? Desire bred lies
As surely as our blindness fuelled their fall.
The thorns of compromise are no great blights —
Better a half-flawed rose than lonely nights.

Dorsington, Warwickshire March 13, 2010

Love is a Loaded Taser

Love is a loaded taser
    Pointed at my heart;
A finger falters... squeezes... fires
A jolt of pain and joy on wires,
To spear me with its razor-
    Sharpened dart.
Love knows nothing of our desires,
Nor cares which corpses crowd its shrine:
Whose finger loosed this bolt of
    Love but mine?

40,000 ft over Greenland   December 9, 2005

taser: trademark: a weapon firing barbs attached
by wires to batteries, causing temporary paralysis.
  — New Oxford Dictionary of English
(Oxford University Press, 1998)

Love's Pledges

Love's pledges must be neither
Too clinging nor too loose,
One suffocates in secret —
One slips the knot to noose.

When promises forge prisons
Love folds her wings from view —
Our ties grow often stronger
Than what we tie them to.

Dorsington, Warwickshire   October 14, 2009

Some Kisses...

Some kisses are like octopi —
    All tearing beak and suction,
While some are moths that flutter by
    On wings of introduction.

Yet others are a mother's balm
    To comfort or to wean us,
Those stolen — burn us like napalm,
    The venomed bite of Venus.

A tipsy aunty's are the worst,
    The bane of what they capture;
The best are hesitant at first —
    Then pave the road to rapture.

Mandalay, Mustique March 28, 2010

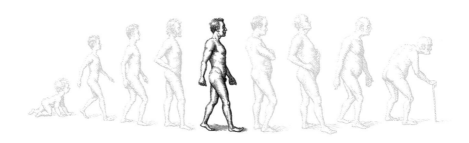

Grown-up

The First Of May

Hooray! Hooray! the first of May,
Outdoor fucking starts today,
But insulate your derriéres
Unless you're ducks or polar bears.

The rain is wet, the wind will freeze
All manner of extremities,
Best wait for June to rut and rout,
And cast no clout 'til May is out!

Dorsington, Warwickshire   May 1, 2011

clout: (noun) archaic
piece of cloth or article of clothing

Yes this poem contains a four-letter word and is about a racy subject, but English poetry has a long tradition of such 'rude' charms, chants and nursery rhymes. If your mother or aunties were told what some of the nursery rhymes they taught to you really meant, they would be blushing furiously!

Oh, The Silk Of Their Flesh

Oh, the silk of their flesh, once hidden beneath
    Those mulberry bushes of plenty,
Their breast on my belly, their tongue in my teeth —
    God! What it was like to be twenty!

Sweet Jenny, Ornella, and Charlotte, and Blaine,
    In beds or on floors or *al fresco*,
The threesomes with Lily and knickerless Jane —
    Now innocent mummies at Tesco!

Dorsington, Warwickshire May 6, 2011

I Shall Be Sorry

I shall be sorry, but I do not care,
And shall not care when we have lain together;
What is sorry? A round mouth shaping air —

Thimbles of air. Well, don't just stand and stare!
Act your age. Untie this bloody tether.
I shall be sorry, though I don't much care

To know you cannot care. But I can bear,
This once, a love as fickle as the weather.
What is a promise? More mouths shaping air.

Hurry, for God's sake. I wonder, will you dare
To beat me black and blue with flesh or leather?
I shall be sorry, but I do not care.

Why should I care when there is nothing there?
The whips of love are lighter than a feather;
What is sorry? A round mouth sobbing air —

A busy thimble — sewing what we tear
From fumbled lives. I cannot tell you whether
I shall be sorry. But I do not care.
What is sorry? A round mouth shaping air.

Dorsington, Warwickshire May 25, 2009

'Downsizing'

The firm's alive with murmurs,
The thrum of gossips din,
The sneers of old long-termers —
Whoever's out — they're in.

No parachutes or rip-cords,
No lifebuoys as she dives,
Fat bastards with their clipboards
Are sharpening their knives.

Receptionists are tearful,
The Boss averts his eye,
'H.R.' is grimly cheerful —
But then — they're paid to lie.

It's meeting, every minute,
It's tackle, grapple, block!
It's 'keep yer 'ead down', innit?
It's in by eight o'clock!

It's straining blood and sinew
To keep abreast of moves:
"The hangings will continue
Until morale improves!"

Mandalay, Mustique January 16, 2002

Soldier Of The Queen

Not very pleasant, is it?
And those who come to visit
Are often in two minds at what they've seen.

There's some as just can't do it,
And others who wade through it,
But none of them are soldiers of the Queen.

We set out late that morning,
No pricking thumbs, no warning,
The sweep around the village seemed routine,

Then BOOM! — they scored a homer!
I cartwheeled into coma,
One legless, luckless soldier of the Queen.

Mind you, I'm not complaining,
And inch by inch I'm gaining
My upper strength to pump like a machine!

Though mirrors leave me weeping,
And though I've trouble sleeping,
The training helps — as soldier of the Queen.

Some say I'm half a man now,
But I do what I can now
To help a mate face up to 'might-have been',

We laugh and sing and drink here,
We don't care what you think here,
Each knowing: we're a soldier of the Queen.

Mandalay, Mustique   August 24, 2013

Written after the singer and photographer, Bryan Adams, showed me the advance photographs and layouts for a book he has been working on for five years called 'Wounded: The Legacy of War'. At first, I could hardly bear to look at these terrifying, unflinching portraits of British service men and women injured in recent wars. Their injuries would make, I believe, even a seasoned surgeon flinch. But gradually, I trained myself to look beyond the missing limbs, burnt flesh, blind eyes and all the rest, to search for the man and woman within the horror of the shell. Their story, too, told in their own words, left me literally in awe at the courage and resilience they so casually exhibit.

A 'homer' is American sports slang for a home run (a big deal - often a game decider) in baseball.

I Have Two Children Now

I have two children now —
A girl and a boy
You never knew,
A husband who loves me—a job I enjoy,
And good friends, too.

I never think of us —
Today at the mart
Was such a shock;
Can ghosts push a cart to the checkout? — my heart
Stopped like a clock.

Dorsington, Warwickshire October 1, 2011

This Little Piggy

This little piggy was burglar,
This little piggy was a thief,
This little piggy broke in my house,
This little piggy came to grief,
This little piggy squealed '*Wee, wee, wee, wee, wee!*
　　He walloped me and now I'll claim relief!
　　A modern thief in no way is naïf!
　　My legal aid will buy a fancy brief!
　　And then I'm off to live in Tenerife!'

Mandalay, Mustique　August 18, 2001

What You Find Out When You're Rich

For one, you become more attractive,
    Acquiring infallible wit,
And for two, your ideas, irrespective
    Of merit, are always a hit.

For three, if you happen to stammer,
    Then others start stammering, too,
And for four, you're amazed to discover
    That so many strangers know *you*.

For five, that the laws of good manners
    Can never apply to the rich,
And six, that of bankers and gangsters,
    Nobody cares which is which.

But the funniest thing about money —
    Speaking as one who should know,
Are those portals, once hidden or bolted,
    That open wherever you go.

Mandalay, Mustique   December 31, 2011

Bits and Bobs

Today, I opened up a drawer jammed shut.
    A faded scent, where bits and bobs were kept,
Reminded me: that grasping, evil slut
    Was once my loving wife. And then, I wept.

Dorsington, Warwickshire April 29, 2010

It Can't Be Done

It can't be done.
I think it can.
It can't be done.
I have a plan.

It can't be done.
I see a way.
It can't be done.
I'll start today.

It can't be done.
I did it, too!
Well that was luck!
(To such as you.)

Dorsington, Warwickshire   May 23, 2010

'Thank You'

To those who nudge and wink, to toad and schemer
    Who earlier had praised you fast enough,
To those who croak: "Another bloody dreamer..."
    And turn away when things are getting tough,
To false fair-weather friends who thought you barmy,
    Each praying you would fail and prove 'em right,
Or Jeremiah fools — that closet army
    Of wretches with no stomach for the fight;

To twenty-twenty hindsight from your lenders
    Who panicked at each petty storm or squall,
To those you once had thought were your defenders,
    But oddly will no longer take your call,
To bottom-feeding scum who would defraud you
    Like pirates, for a penny in the pound,
Or those who speak of life-boats as they board you
    To rob you just the second you're aground;

To Nightmare and his cohorts that come creeping
    In fevered dreams of loss beyond repair,
To thudding heart and night sweats as you're sleeping
    While Fear incites fresh servants of Despair,
To doubts that stride by daylight to assail you
    And stop your mouth with thoughts of the abyss,
Or siren sighs whose whisperings impale you:
    "My dearest, I implore you, drop all this..."

To ghouls who cram their gullets with your winnings
    And pass the bottle round in loud salute,
To creeps who claim they 'nurtured your beginnings',
    (A bone they tossed, and grudgingly, to boot),
To those who claim your bed, your gifts, your riches
    Now Lady Luck has brought you safe to port,
Say 'thank you' — as you bless the sons-of-bitches
    For every rotten trick the buggers taught!

Dorsington, Warwickshire April 21, 2011

White Van Man

(To the tune of Old King Cole)

White Van Man has a very white van
    And a very white van has he,
Except for the dents and the rust by the vents
    And some very rude Graf-ee-tee.

He drives in his van as fast as he can
    And he neither hears nor sees,
He clings to his phone like a dog with a bone
    While he steers with one of his kneeeees.

He picks his nose while the tailback grows
    And yacks to his front-seat crew,
But a fool so rash as to honk or flash
    Will receive the fingers twooooo.

Oh, White Van man has a very wide clan
    Who profess no Highway Code,
They'll shunt your rear and yell in your ear
    As they U-turn in the roooooad.

He stamps on his brakes when he overtakes
    As he cuts up you and me,
For White Van Man has a very white van...
    And a very white van has heeeee!

Dorsington, Warwickshire   June 28, 2005

Leaving Sex Out Of This

Leaving sex out of this
There are few physical exertions more satisfying than
Taking an urgent piss
On virgin snow, or lighting up a really good cigar,
Or lifting the first glass
Of nectar to your eager lips while leaning over the bar
To pat the barmaid's arse,
Or slotting an impossible shot — *bam!* — into a pocket
Your mates had bet you'd miss,
Or bolting two hot dogs with mustard down your gob at the game.
Leaving sex out of this.

Dorsington, Warwickshire March 13, 2010

'This is the Server...'

I

This is the Server, waiting on station,
Silicone god of an e-mail nation,

Bearing you news of a baby boy,
Bringing you misery, bringing you joy —

Telling you auntie has taken to pottery,
Gloating your ex has won the lottery,

Jottings ethereal, letters venereal,
Packets attaching the oddest material,

Bleating that Katie has married a fool,
Reminding you "Man' United rule!"

Enclosing a last demand from creditors,
Filing a blast to newspaper editors,

Begging the pardon of furious lovers,
Shopping for pillows and sofa covers,

Juggling schedules, checking arrivals,
Flattering bosses, flattening rivals,

Laden with rumours and odious jokes
Featuring zebras and artichokes...

II

Servant of presidents, servant of hacks,
Blinking and winking in towering stacks,

Serving up poetry, panic and porn,
Dishing the dirt from dusk til dawn,

Guarding the gospels of new messiahs,
Tracking the passage of forest fires,

Plotting an expedition to Everest,
Funding your local neighbourhood terrorist,

Bidding for first editions of Keats,
Cribbing your homework, booking your seats,

Checking if Daddy has taken his medicine,
Clinching the date of birth for Edison,

Gathering evidence, paying your taxes,
Ordering pizza and beer from Max's,

Auctioning Fords and a red Mercedes,
(All of them owned by little old ladies),

Shooting the breeze and playing at *Doom*,
A long-legged fly in a steel-racked room...

III

The Server has crashed!
The Server is down!
The screens have dimmed in city and town,
The emperor stripped of his digital gown,
The babbling web is lame and halt,
Its pillars of Silicone ground to salt —
Default! Default!
Default! Default!

The Server is up!
The Server is back!
The techies have purged a hacker attack,
The natter and chatter is back on track,
The terminal drives have held their nerve,
The Server survives — and as you observe —
I serve! I serve!
I serve! I serve!

Mandalay, Mustique   April 27, 2003

(With fond acknowledgement
to W.H. Auden's great poem
'Night Train' which served as
the inspiration for this poem.)

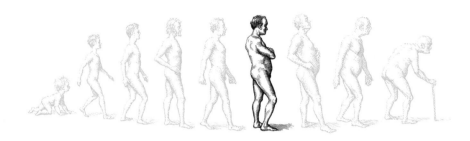

Reflections

Because

Because men's pride is stronger than their purpose
    When pride is all they have, or all they've known,
Because the praise of others makes us nervous
    (For men are what they are, not what they own);
Because our tinsel trappings drive us blindly
    And 'way leads on to way' — and habits stick;
Because we love success, but not too kindly,
    And seek her out, but fear to learn the trick;

Because our lives are short — yet complicated,
    And raging at the gods is infantile,
Because our whims and sins are automated,
    Or buried in the tyranny of style;
Because there are no secrets worth the keeping
    And Keepers claim the Fifth — if ever pressed;
Because the Fourth Estate is busy sleeping,
    (An advertiser clutched to either breast);

Because the wolves of law are smooth-tongued liars
    With pimps in sober robes to rob and fleece,
Because our bandaged hands must stoke the fires,
    And bureaucrats will never hold their peace,
Because our Men of God are — politicians,
    Who render unto Caesar what is due;
Because we fill our children with ambitions
    To mirror what we say, not what we do;

Because we shield our eyes from other's loathing,
    And hide away the follies of our youth,
Because we choose the label — not the clothing,
    And substitute bad manners for the truth;
Because we mourn the crowd, yet shun seclusion
    For fear a voice may whisper what we're worth,
Because men damn free will as mere illusion:
    We walk the paths — predestined from our birth.

Mandalay, Mustique January 6, 2003

I Bit The Hand That Fed Me

I bit the hand that fed me,
And bled it in my grip,
The left was held in friendship —
His right concealed a whip.

The faithless fool still curses,
He calls us dogs and curs,
But I have learned from horses —
Too many Men love spurs.

Dorsington, Warwickshire   July 21, 2010

Blood Brother

Wherever you are, whatever you've done,
   However the land is lying,
If you but call by night or day,
Though hope is lost and the Devil to pay,
Though hounds of hell should bar the way,
Yet I would come to where you lay —
   Or perish in the trying.

Wherever you are, whatever you've done,
   Whichever the flag you're flying,
If but you call by day or night,
In men's contempt, in friend's despite,
By the sickle moon or broad daylight,
Yet I shall come to set all right —
   Or perish in the trying.

Dorsington, Warwickshire   November 20, 2002

Do Not Ask Me To Look Skyward

Do not ask me to look skyward — you grew up
In rooms with fitted carpets. I did not.
Nor did I read the tea leaves in my cup,
My eyes were peeled for vomit, turds and snot
In alleyways, guiding my shoeless feet
To safer ground. Oh, it's easy to wax wise
Or emulate philosophy's conceit
With bellies full of wine and star-strewn skies.
Mind you, a lapcat's purr is bought too dear,
The product of some owner's whips and bells —
Your cheerful sermons grate upon the ear
For those of us who trudge the lower hells...
  So as you praise the moon, mind how you go,
  A stone may stub your silver-sandalled toe!

Mandalay, Mustique August 2, 2013

I hear Conservative Party supporters bemoaning the fact that so few people realise what a decent chap David Cameron is. They are the same crew who cannot understand why Jamie Oliver has been pilloried for lecturing the so-called 'working classes' for spending money on large screen televisions and not on healthy food. I know they mean well (well, at least I feel Mr. Oliver does) but unless you have lived — as I have done — on the margin of your society, with little or no money at all, uncertain where your next meal will come from and dreading being tossed out on the street because you cannot pay the rent — unless you have experienced searching for work and not finding it and having to endure the kindness of friends buying you a drink which you cannot reciprocate — unless you have experienced this, you would do well to be very careful before opining on the fecklessness of the poor and offering unwanted and often offensive advice. End of sermon.

House Rules

We play in the House of Original Sin,
Where the name of the game is Blame,
Where Habit and Guilt take turns to spin
And credit is measured in Shame;
Where the wheel is rigged, the fix is in,
And the rules stay always the same:
You cannot break even; you cannot win;
And you cannot get out of the game.

Mandalay, Mustique   July 19, 2003

In the three principal Laws of Thermodynamics, (there are four, but we needn't go into that), the First states that energy cannot be created, the Second that some energy is always wasted (no perpetual motion possible) and the Third that you can never reduce temperatures to absolute zero. As Bill Bryson notes in his A Short History of Nearly Everything (Doubleday 2003), these laws are sometimes expressed jocularly by physicists as follows: (1) you can't win, (2) you can't break even, and (3) you can't get out of the game. This struck me as a sound summation for the human condition, never mind thermodynamics!

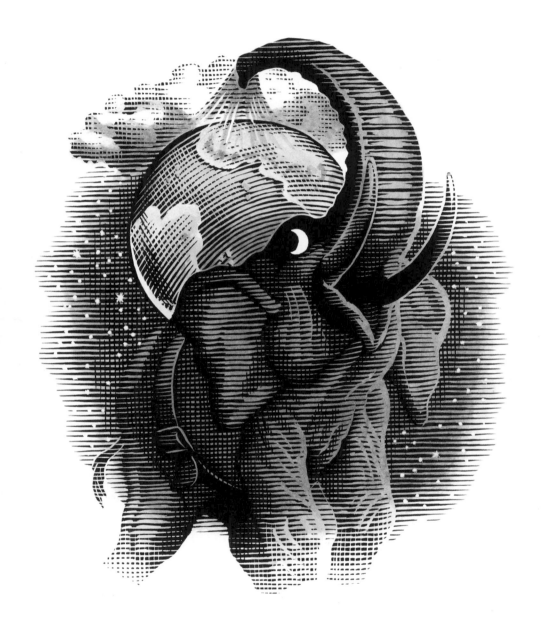

'An elephant carries a ball on his back...'

An elephant carries a ball on his back,
He circles the sun with the stars for a track,
He swings to the left, he swings to the right,
And the ants on the ball call it morning and night.

An elephant carries a ball on his back,
And if he should trumpet — the continents crack!
When he glides on the edge of his shadowy wing
The ants on the ball call it winter or spring.

An elephant carries a ball on his back,
His tongue is a sunset of scarlet and black,
When he waggles an ear there is storm or typhoon,
And the ants on the ball think his eye is the moon.

An elephant carries a ball on his back,
And once in a while his saddle grows slack,
It scrapes on his belly, which leads him to sneeze
And the ants on the ball tumble down on their knees.

An elephant carries a ball on his back,
He circles the sun with the stars for a track,
His trunk is the fount of the rain and the mist —
But the ants on the ball say he doesn't exist!

Mandalay, Mustique February 27, 2006

Dedicated with tolerant affection to religious Creationists and their latest acolyte — so-called 'Intelligent Design' which is of course, in its turn, (surprise, surprise!) the old 'Eternal Watchmaker' theory, brought up to date in the sheep's clothing of junk science. Nice try, guys, but no cigar.

None Of Us Are As Special As We Think

None of us are as special as we think.
Nor as unimportant as some say.
Opinion's puffed-up toads, when prodded, shrink.

What can we know as players in the play?
The audience — if there is one — lost to sight.
Each one of us was born an émigré,

Not knowing where we came from. Life's swift flight,
Accelerates, like gravity, to earth
With little time to ponder on our plight.

Our petty hurts, when seen for what they're worth,
Are drops that fill Creation's sea; they sink
Beneath the ageless waves of joy and birth.

When troubles come, seek out the stars and wink.
None of us are as special as we think.

Dorsington, Warwickshire May 7, 2011

Sonnets are a short form of poetry. They nearly always contain fourteen lines, but the rules of stanza formation, rhyme, meter and so on can be very different from one sonnet to the next. There are rules, however. Generally, sonnet's are split into two types: (1) English (or Shakespearian or Spenserian) sonnets or (2) Italian (or Petrarchan) sonnets. The latter are the older form. The rhyme schemes at the end of lines varies, but both forms share an underlying structure — the first part of the poem introduces the reader to an idea, an argument, mood or debate... while the second part of the poem attempts to resolve (or at least to make sense of) the first part. The sonnet above falls into neither of the two main categories, and is therefore a 'broken' sonnet.

Martyrs

All martyrs share a Janus face
    To stare both ways — at peace, at war,
Compassion learns her proper place:
    A beggar by a bolted door.

    Beware when true believers call,
    Gods may die and empires fall,
    As donkeys nod and zealots bawl:
    Damn all martyrs, damn them all!

The souls of righteousness appear
    To seek fresh kindling of their own,
Blind faith sneers at a parent's tear
    For pious sons with hearts of stone.

    Beware when true believers call,
    Gods may die and empires fall,
    Best to turn and face the wall:
    Damn all martyrs, damn them all!

Mandalay, Mustique July 23, 2013

Janus was the ancient Roman god who kept the gate of heaven. He was represented with two faces, one facing forward and one behind. The doors of his temple were kept open in time of war and closed during times of peace.

The Law That Knows No Law

Behold the law that rules the fates
    Of all men — rich or poor;
A law that shapes our loves and hates,
That starves us out or heaps our plates,
A law that smirks at men's debates,
    A law that knows no law —

A law bereft of pity,
A law that knows no sleep,
A law that heeds no prayer or deed,
A law that none may keep.

Behold the law that marks the slates
    Of kings and men of straw;
That raises fools while wise men grope,
Throws wide or bars the gates of hope,
That tabulates each inch of rope,
    A law that knows no law —

A law that conjures music
While moons and men must dance,
Whose iron rods rule apes and gods:
Behold! The Law of Chance.

Dorsington, Warwickshire   November 15, 2002

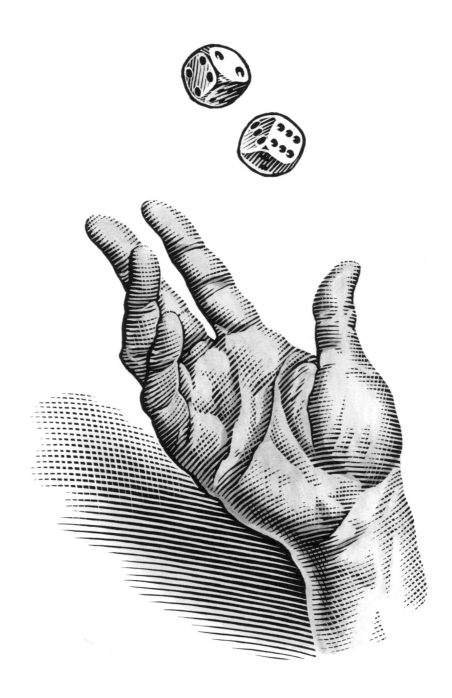

A 'man of straw' is an expression for a person (often in a business or legal sense) who turns out not to be as well off or as solvent as they first appear. Thus, to sue a man of straw to get your money back is yet more good money poured down the drain. As to the 'law of chance' there is no such thing, scientifically or mathematically speaking. No computer or piece of software currently known can produce utterly random results or choices. Nor can humans do so, because our brains are conditioned to perceive in patterns. Without perfect randomness there cannot be a scientific law of chance, although, in practise, we can get very, very close to it!

Of Paradise

If it were left to men or mice
To conjure their own paradise —
If elephants or witless fleas
Were masters of eternities —
What fool would wish to wake each day
Where tigers hunt undying prey,
Or in a world where Fat Joe scoffs
His cakes from everlasting troughs,
Where Bogie struts in black and white
Through Casablanca every night,
Or worse, where adolescence reigns
And spotters tick off deathless trains
While virgins bearing ice-cold beer
Sing sweet endearments in their ear?
If it were left to such as these,
To mice or men or witless fleas,
Then we should learn, perhaps too well,
The truest measurement — of hell,
Where one man's fantasy of wit
For others, emulates the pit.

Mandalay, Mustique   August 24, 2004

Retribution

The Semtex strapped around him,
His heart devoid of fear,
'Allahu Akbar! God is Great!
And paradise stands near.
I wreak His vengeance here!'

A schoolboy kicks his classmate,
The blow repaid in kind.
'Eye for an eye' we teach them;
One day the world will find,
All humankind gone blind.

Mandalay, Mustique   January 20, 2001

(My thanks to Dana Gillespie whose quote from
Mahatma Gandhi in the last line inspired the above.)

'I do not know who made me...'

I do not know who made me,
Still less do I care,
The sheep that dot the meadow
Make no altar there.

Of transubstantiation
Beetles never learn,
The foxes build no bonfires
Where heretics must burn.

The bees that gather honey
Propagate in sin,
Nor do they slay in *jihad*
Their unbelieving kin.

No missionary weasels
Slither on the sly,
Nor does the dormouse tell me
That I must kneel or die.

Your words are your opinions,
Who knows what is true?
I do not know who made me —
And neither, friend, do you.

Dorsington, Warwickshire   October 8, 2006

'The world would be astonished if it knew how great a proportion of its brightest ornaments, of those most distinguished even in popular estimation for wisdom and virtue, are complete sceptics in religion.'
— John Stuart Mill (1806 - 1873), English essayist and philosopher, who quite certainly included himself in such a 'proportion'.

Transubstantiation is a Catholic doctrine that the whole substance of the bread and wine changes into the substance of the body and blood of Christ when consecrated in the Eucharist. This doctrine is rejected by Protestants.

Jihad: a holy war against infidels undertaken by Muslims in defence of Islamic faith.

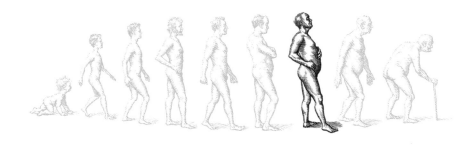

Ripe

Before — and After

When you're young — they want you older,
When you're old — they want you young;
When she's gone — you wish you'd told her,
When she's back — you bite your tongue.

When you're cross — its *'Let's not fight, dear,'*
When you're tired — it's party time!
When you're hard — it's *'Not tonight, dear,'*
When you're prose — she speaks in rhyme.

When you're broke — it's *'I've been thinking...'*
When you're rich — it's *'...join the gym!'*
When you're ill — its *'...all that drinking...'*
When you're dead — it's *'Who? Oh, him!'*

Mandalay, Mustique   December 18, 2003

'I built myself a house of wood...'

I built myself a house of wood
Where once an apple orchard stood.
On stormy nights I lay in bed
While rafters moaned above my head.

They wept aloud for limbs long lost,
For buds pinched out by early frost,
For wicker baskets piled with fruit,
For phantom branch and withered root.

I caulked the roof and rafter beams,
But still they whispered in my dreams,
They spoke of rising sap and wood:
And then, at last, I understood.

This spring, I planted out a score
Of apple saplings by my door.
Now stormy nights my rafters chime
To cider choirs and nursery rhyme.

Mandalay, Mustique   May 6, 2003

'I sleep alone...'

I sleep alone... to loosen tongue-tied joints,
   (My body lies too still for company),
Its rag doll limbs adrift like compass points.
   I sleep alone... because I need to be.

I sleep alone... because I sometimes fart,
   Because I lie awake in shiftless drift,
My mind astride the hoof-beats of my heart,
   I sleep alone... to hide a grievous gift.

I sleep alone... to snore, and cough, and read,
   To vivisect old demons in the dark.
My savage dreams accustomed to their need,
   I sleep alone... lest hidden fuses spark.

I sleep alone... to shield myself from shame,
   To stifle panic's press in privacy,
Each sweated cloth a winding sheet of flame,
   I sleep alone... so none shall ever see.

I sleep alone... though once, in lightfoot youth,
   Our beds were rendezvous for idle lust,
And if I miss your silk-soft flesh — in truth,
   I sleep alone, my dear, because I must.

Mandalay, Mustique January 17, 2004

Few Eyes Are Innocent

Few eyes are innocent — the gaze
Of any infant grades and weighs
Each looming face for ill intent,
While miles away a hawk has spent
Its morning quartering a hill
To scry a vole — to stoop and kill.

In meeting rooms, lean hawks in suits
Lock glances as their substitutes
Debate the toss — or shift their ground:
An eyeblink, and we lose the round!
While far away, in foreign skies,
A silent drone sprouts thermal eyes.

A warrior's vacant ten-mile stare
Has failed to spot death hovering there;
The flirting looks of brides-to-be
Weave snares within their mystery;
Geronimo grants his parole
While cameras stole his people's soul...

Few eyes are innocent, yet who
Dares view their own — as others do?

Mandalay, Mustique   August 9, 2010

I Have Wasted the Day

I have wasted the day in the fields and the lanes,
    I have tramped in the leaves and the mud;
I have dined upon air and scrumped me a pear
    And an apple the colour of blood.

Though my fingers are purple from blackberry stains,
    Though my hair is a tangle of straw;
Though my jacket was torn upon bramble and thorn,
    It was worth it for all that I saw.

It was worth all the aches, it was worth all the pains —
    I have rambled and scrambled and raced;
And my stick was mislaid where I dozed in the shade,
And I waded in brooks and neglected my books,
And I startled a hare (and the *taste* of that pear!)
    What waste, what a glorious waste!

Dorsington, Warwickshire September 29, 2002

Sunday September 29, 2002 was just such a day — an autumnal day when it was good to be alive; when the hedgerows and trees were bursting with fruit, when the sun shone, when the wind was mild, when the leaves on the trees glowed like miniature sunsets, when birds sang and silly squirrels foraged for nuts... the kind of day when only an invalid, a prisoner or an idiot would not have stolen a few hours in what is left of the English countryside. So I did!

Plan For The Future

Plan for the future, live in the now,
Ration the past, but never allow
Memory's will-o'-the-wisp to praise
The sanctity of 'the good old days'.

ALTERNATE VERSION:

Plan For The Future

Plan for the future —
Ration the past —
Live in the present —
Nothing can last
Other than miscreant
Memory's haze,
Glossing the rot of
The 'good old days'

Mandalay, Mustique May 25, 2013

I have included two versions of this poem. A very famous poet once remarked that a poem is never 'finished'; it is only 'finished with' by its author. Many poets have constantly revised their work. The most famous reviser of all was the American poet Walt Whitman (1819-1892) who often spent decades revising his poems, to the delight of later poetry professors and scholars and the despair of publishers and English Literature students.

Why not attempt your own version of the idea behind this poem on the blank page opposite? (Hint: if you use a pencil, you can always rub out a botched attempt and try again!)

Plan For The Future

The Oldest Error

To My 'Green' Friends

I love the earth, therefore the earth loves me.
You great green-hearted booby! All such stuff
Neglects what any fool knows well enough
Who farms the land or sails a treacherous sea.
We are no alien interlopers here;
Earth loves us neither more nor less than sheep,
Or marmosets or monsters of the deep.
We eat because our forbears dined on fear
And found it insufficient to their needs.
Fair nature sets few feasts for those she breeds,
Nor smiles to hear your Jeremiah groans —
This phantom lover soon will grind your bones
    As she has ground all others, hale or halt.
    Love nature all you please — but pass the salt.

Dorsington, Warwickshire   April 8, 2010

The title and first line of this poem comes from a short essay by Richard Jeffries written in the 1880s. Jeffries was one of the finest writers on nature who ever lived. His bleak, heart-wrenching observations on the English countryside are well worth reading today. As to my many 'green' friends — I ask them, once again, to recall that Mother Nature has neither asked for nor requires their help. She is indifferent and perfectly able to look after herself. As a species, we must either learn to reduce our numbers and live sensibly or we shall be destroyed. (Perhaps a few may escape to migrate elsewhere if technology permits.) But nature could care less. Like the 'gods', or 'fate', 'destiny', or the 'afterlife', 'nature' is no more than an anthropomorphic invention of human fears and desires.

Unsung Heroes

For those who never found it too much trouble
　　To help their fellow man — nor asked the price,
For those who wield their shovels in the rubble
　　While scholars scoff at building paradise;
For those who fetch and carry for their neighbours,
　　Or wash the sick or sit beside the frail,
For those who earn a pittance for their labours,
　　But never play the martyred tattletale:

For those for whom a word of thanks suffices,
　　Or deem that it was meant, if never said,
For those who run a mile from fame's devices,
　　And hide their medals underneath the bed;
For those who slave in worn out wards and clinics,
　　Or work beside the nurses, hand in glove,
For those who pay no mind to whining cynics,
　　Who know the worth, if not the price, of love:

For those who give their lives to teaching others,
　　Yet never learn the meaning of conceit,
For those who treat the homeless as their brothers,
　　For men who empty bins and sweep the street;
For volunteers who listen — but don't lecture,
　　For coppers who would rather wear no gun,
For juries who can cast aside conjecture
　　And steel themselves to do what must be done:

For friends who keep their temper, yet stay candid,
　　For citizens who stand up to the yobs,
For those who bring up children single-handed,
　　For companies who tailor-make them jobs;
For those who blew the whistle as they hung us,
　　For those who stood when you and I would fall,
For these, the unsung heroes here among us:
　　Please raise your glass to bless them, one and all.

Dorsington, Warwickshire June 1, 2003

'We are different when we are alone...'

We are different when we are alone,
    When artifice has no use,
When the mask of our laughter is bone
    And the werewolf of self is loose;

As fingernails harden to claws
    And skin to reptilian scale,
As we lope to our bed on all fours,
    And the mirror reveals a tail...

With the birds of community flown,
    We to ourselves grow strange,
We are different when we are alone —
    Like a garden at night, we change.

Dorsington, Warwickshire May 28, 2005

'Kohl'

Our big, black, faithful dog has died,
I found him, lying on his side
Splayed on the rug, beside the bed:
Our big, black, faithful dog is dead.

Never a whimper, never a whine,
His coat like midnight, eyes a-shine,
A lion's heart, a fool to bribe,
The gentleman of all his tribe.

My lover's friend, and my friend, too,
Has gone — as we bid Kohl adieu
And many a foolish tear is shed:
Our big, black, faithful dog is dead.

Mandalay, Mustique   August 10, 2006

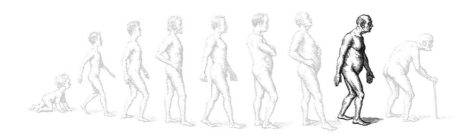

Over-the-hill

Grand-ma

Today he calls me 'grand-ma',
    My hair as white as snow,
But that's not what he called me
    Near fifty year ago;
My curls a fiery tangle,
    My skin a slick of sweat,
My lover riding bare-back
    And we just only met!

When next you're with your grand-ma,
    Try closing half an eye,
Smooth out the wrinkled creases,
    Add lipstick on the sly,
Imagine fiery tresses,
    Imagine there's no dress!
Then save your pity, dearie —
    Been there — done that. Oh yes!

Mandalay, Mustique   February 2, 2002

129

I Meet A Stranger In The Glass

I meet a stranger in the glass
Each morning when I rise,
Two half-familiar eyes stare back
In mystified surprise.

I ask the stranger, 'Please remove
The mask of what I knew,'
Occasionally they blink or shed
A salty tear or two.

Betrayal is too strong a word
But lives are each betrayed —
By sagging flesh or broken hopes —
By promises unmade.

A looking-glass is proof emough,
Its stranger conjures truth,
If you are young, you're rich! Be wise
And revel in your youth!

Mandalay, Mustique   July 30, 2013

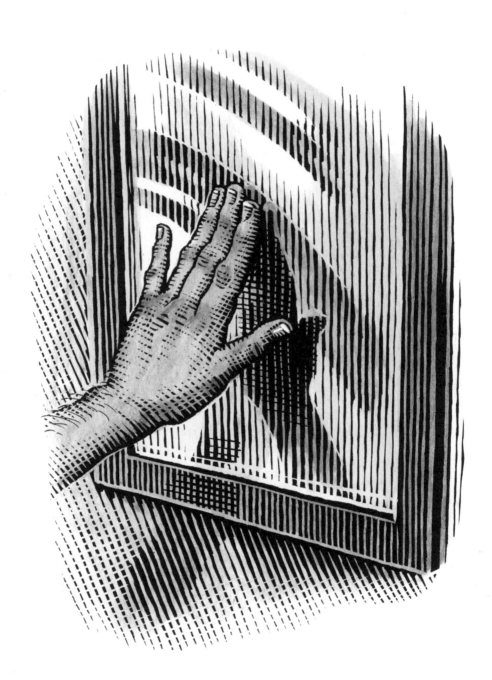

Just Passing

We were just passing, so I said to Jack,
'Let's look him up.' We found the house and knocked.
No dice. I thought, 'We'll just check round the back.

And here you are. Oh, such a beautifully stocked
Garden — and comfy chairs on a striped lawn.
It's been years. Years! I hope you aren't too shocked!'

Startled perhaps, but not too much to mourn
The pink-lipped, wide-eyed waif who bedded me —
What, forty years ago? Her ringlets shorn,

The slight breasts blotted out of memory,
The flawless skin grown coarse — the slim neck slack
Where once my vampire gnawing made so free,

Her long legs scissored round my sweat-slicked back.
'We were just passing, so I said to Jack...'

Dorsington, Warwickshire March 15, 2010

Que Sera Sera

I'd bloody swear they weren't there yesterday.
Not that I search for them, exactly. Oh!
There's another! You see more when you know
Just what to look for. God! it's *white*, not gray,
Wiry. Like a malignant stowaway.
I'm scarcely *thirty*. Well, thirty-five or so,
And what's that, after all? I've heard fools crow:
'The age that youth surrenders to its prey',
Well, *they* can surrender all they want. Not me.
Middle-aged men do not offend the eye;
And are often called 'distinguished'. Not so we,
Who scarcely face a glass without a sigh.
    Sod *que sera sera* and what must be:
    I'm off to the shops to buy myself some dye!

Dorsington, Warwickshire March 17, 2010

'I plucked all the cherries...'

I plucked all the cherries
Chance would allow,
Take them, and welcome —
I'm done with them now.

Done with the ladder
And done with the tree,
Take them, and welcome —
They're no use to me.

Done with the getting of
What I could get,
Take it, and welcome —
Try not to forget

To pluck all the cherries
Chance will allow,
Take them, and welcome —
I'm done with them now.

Mandalay, Mustique   August 8, 2006

'The world is round...'

The world is round. But not to me.
We each see what we want to see —
Tho' science shows horizons bent
Full circle, or a few percent
In colour photographs. But still,
Portray the damn thing how you will,
To me the world is thorny-hedged
With wire fences, razor-edged,
And in the meadow, fruit and vine,
And by the gate an ugly sign;
And in the stream a speckled trout
That men may watch but not fish out;
And in the woods are pheasants, too,
But these are not for me or you
With keepers spying round each tree.
The world is round. But not to me.

If wolves were born without the wish
To guzzle from a porcelain dish,
The rich are born with silk and spurs,
And sep'rate bathrooms, 'His and Hers',
While in their towers, wolves in suits
Export the jobs of men in boots
Without so much as 'by your leave'
So kiddies here must learn to thieve —
Not though they needed teaching much,
I'll grant you that, with drugs and such,
And gangsta sluts and rapper gits
Or has-beens flashing out their tits
On TV every other night:
No wonder kids think its their 'right'
To own each bloody thing they see —
The world is round. But not to me.

And I'm a fool. And old. And poor,
And don't know what an iPod's for,
I buys me bits at market stalls
And never visits shopping malls
And still votes Labour — God knows why
When all the bastards do is lie
And leave us here to rot and shrink —
There's more of us than you might think,
Who live in mortal fear of debt
And never surfed the internet,
With bitter hearts and brittle bones
And thumbs too fat for modern phones,
Who find it hard to understand
Who wrecked our green and pleasant land.
There's something rotten here. You'll see.
The world is round. But not to me.

Dorsington, Warwickshire   May 8, 2005

The Rill Of Hope

What feeds this feeble rill of Hope
Trickling to a Lake of Doubt?
Whose servants march beside its slope
Whispering of dams and drought?

From beck to brook, from brook to streams,
To cataracts of roiling grief
Which thunder through our fevered dreams
To drown in pools of disbelief...

What nourishment from depthless wells.
From sunless seas — what nameless source
Dares circumscribe our private hells
To bid our helmsman: 'Hold your course!'

When all is lost, when terror reigns
And men despair — when deaths are cures
And rope the remedy for pains:
Still, drop by drop, Hope's rill endures!

Dorsington, Warwickshire January 31, 2012

Without hope we are nothing. This is another poem written shortly after the confirmation of the diagnosis of my throat cancer back in January 2012. I like Leonard Cohen's take on this subject. He once quipped: 'Sure, there is a crack in everything. That's how the light gets in.'

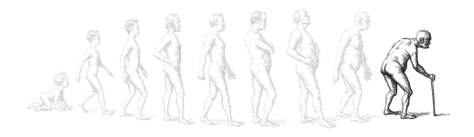

Endings

Adieu!

Chance makes brothers but hearts make friends,
Here then, before our friendship ends
As now it must, my friend, be glad
For what we shared — for what we had.

How late we learn, how little we knew
Of those who stood, blade-straight, steel-true,
To brace when push had come to shove:
Chance makes brothers — but hearts make love!

Candlewood Lake, Connecticut   October 23, 2012

Goodbye! Goodbye!

The martins are preparing their goodbyes,
Their swooping flutter fills the autumn skies,
They chitter by my head as if to say:
'Thanks for the nesting site, but we're away!
The soft lands in the south have warmth to spare,
And we have felt a chill upon the air,
Our young are fledged, the flock is on the wing!
Goodbye! Goodbye!
       We'll see you in the spring!'

Dorsington, Warwickshire September 5, 2013

The saddest day of the year for me is when the house-martins join the swallows in a great circling arc around my house in late September or early October, twittering and chittering in flocks one hundred or two hundred strong. Both the fit and mature as well as the weak and adolescent must now make a long perilous journey from which scarcely half will emerge to enjoy the English winter in the 'soft south' of Spain or Africa. What a journey for such tiny creatures! How brutal nature is in its relentless selection of the survival of the fittest. And how empty our skies are here in Warwickshire for half the year! I wrote this poem while watching the martins and swallows 'practise' their flying and acrobatic skills and building their strength for the great trial to come.

'I am listening, now...'

I am listening, now. The past is past,
I'm here. I'm sitting beside your bed.
Speak to me now. It's time at last
To make amends. The past is dead.

I am listening, now. I'm here, my dear.
Your spotted hands are soft as fur.
Speak to me, now. I've ears to hear,
They are not so deaf as once they were.

I am listening, now. I'm done with fuss;
Babble of treachery, love or pain,
Speak of yourself, of them, of us —
Speak of the ghosts that fill the rain.

I am listening, now. I left it late,
Later than ever we thought or knew.
Speak to me. Please. Unbar the gate.
Turn back, my dear. I'm here for you.

Mandalay, Mustique January 25, 2005

'...but the rain is full of ghosts tonight...'
  — Edna St. Vincent Millay

146

'I found a cat...'

I found a cat — knife thin,
So thin it could not live another week,
Or so it seemed. It's skin
A mat of mange, dead eyes, a ravaged cheek.
Yet here it curls today, content and sleek.

I found a coin — and sought
To breed it with another. Year by year,
I traded, sold and caught
The coins of other men, bought cheap or dear.
And here they glint today, stacked tier on tier.

I found a friend — the kind
Who lifts the heart with banter, wit and mirth,
Whose laughing eyes were blind
To fault or flaw, perceiving only worth.
My friend lies here today, beneath the earth.

Cat, coin or friend —
        immutable as clay.
All life's a kiln —
        enjoy it while you may.

Dorsington, Warwickshire
November 22, 2008

This is the Song

This is the song that none can sing,
This is the gift the old gods bring,
Sung this once as the soul takes wing
In the emptiness of night.

Here is the powerlessness of speech,
The letting go that none can teach,
The song of things beyond our reach
Singing to its own light.

Mandalay, Mustique   April 9, 2007

I Will Meet You There

As the veil of life's unmaking
Ravels up its thread,
At the moment of your waking,
When all dreams have fled,

Should there come a distant cry,
Or the echo of a name,
It is I — my dearest — *I!*
Though the sky itself is flame,

Though the hills are oceans breaking
In that last despair,
At the moment of your waking —
I will meet you there.

Candlewood, Connecticut June 30, 2008

On Watching My Mother Die

I am no good at this — as bold men creep
From rooms where women dress and lay the dead,
I find that I have made excuse, or fled
When duty bids me face what makes us weep.
Cowardice then, for fear I delve too deep
Within those woods where bitter tears are shed,
Beside those crags where hunters dare not tread
And only wounded hinds attempt the leap.
Here is a lone wolf — long fled from the pack,
Who fears no mortal hurt or living thing;
Yet now, this flood of feeling swamps the track
Where I had thought to wander until spring —
  'I am no good...' I catch her flickered eye
  '...at this...' A smile, a hoarse reply: *'Nor I!'*

Dorsington, Warwickshire   April 14, 2009

However, my mother did not die — to the astonishment of doctors and everyone else, she recovered from her stroke and is still alive and very much kicking as I type this in early 2014.

Whispered the Rowan to the Oak

The woods of our youth are failing,
        even the mightiest rot,
Beetle and high wind take them
        and soon they will be forgot,
Yet sadder than even the fading
        of suns too eager to set
Is that you should fail to remember
        what I can never forget.

Saplings of strangers surround us
        to feather the winter sky,
Yet though you survive beside me,
        you see with an empty eye,
Far better we fall and nourish
        the land in a last duet
Than that you should fail to remember
        what I can never forget.

Mandalay, Mustique January 1, 2007

To become senile is a terrifying process, not just for the victim, but for those who care for him or her. In the end, death comes to all things that live — a bristle cone pine tree in the Sierra Nevada may survive 5,000 years while you, gentle reader will have done well if you pass your 90th birthday. But senility of any sort is a kind of living death, sickening every thing and every one who comes into contact with it. I have seen it met with courage and fortitude and good humour. But it is a fate I would not wish upon my worst enemy.

A Child By My Deathbed

(Where She Knew She Did Not Ought To Be)

Sit if you wish to —
    Silence is wearing,
    Here I lie staring
        Still as a stone;
Tell you a secret?
    Why do you pry, dear?
    No need to cry, dear —
        Tell me your own!

If I have secrets
    They shall stay with me,
    You must forgive me,
        Curious miss,
Go when you'd like to,
    Don't beg my pardon!
    Off to the garden —
        Leave me a kiss.

Mandalay, Mustique February 24, 2014

Acknowledgements

This book was suggested to me by Gail Rebuck, head of Random House, in late 2012 and commissioned by Cathy Rentzenbrink of 'Quick Reads' in early 2013. 'Quick Reads' is a charitable venture designed to encourage reading. Despite initial enthusiasm for the completed manuscript, 'Quick Reads' felt that some of the poems were unsuitable for their target audience. I was reluctant to amend or omit them so we parted company. I am grateful to Ebury for good-naturedly shrugging off this false start and offering to publish the book as it stood and stands. If, as Shelley once claimed, poets are the 'unacknowledged legislators of the world', I doubt I shall ever be asked to act as a diplomat on English poetry's behalf. On the other hand, such has rarely been the role of poets down the ages. The word 'poet', after all, comes via an old French word — descending from Latin and originally from an ancient Greek word for 'maker'. Neither 'moderator' nor 'censor' play any part in this etymology.

I extend grateful thanks to Gail Rebuck at Random House, for the initial idea for this book, and Fiona MacIntyre and Carey Smith at Ebury Publishing for so generously offering to publish it. Caroline Rush oversaw each stage of this book's production and Rebecca Jezzard has designed it beautifully. The illustrations throughout the book are the work of Bill Sanderson. Britain's finest colour book printer, Butler, Tanner & Dennis in Frome, are printing the book and George Taylor composed the music for the accompanying CD and produced and organised my studio voice recordings. Thanks, also, to Rosemary Bailey for casting her editorial eye over the text and eliminating numerous typographical errors. In addition, Don Atyeo and Moni Mannings, my readers, are invaluable in their observations, as is Simon Rae, who has been my ad hoc editor for many years.

Mick Watson, Thom Stretton and Scott Watson at Class Act ensure that when I am on the road my readings are at least technical *tours de force*. Toby Fisher, Wendy Kasabian, Steve Kotok, Catherine Law, Lloyd Warren, and a cast of what sometimes seems like thousands play their heroic parts while, back at the ranch, Ian Leggett, Andrew Boyd, Selena Robinson, Lance Welch, Michael Hyman, David Bliss, Cathy Galt and her team, keep the home fires burning. Jonathan Noone is the guardian of my gargantuan website **www.felixdennis.com** where nearly all of my poetry — amongst much else — can be read, heard and even viewed on video. Jerina Hardy handles my PR. Lastly, as always, I thank the companion of my heart, Marie-France Demolis.

Index

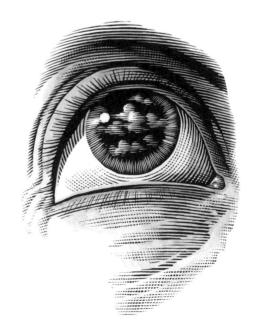

Felix Dennis

Felix Dennis is one of Britain's best-loved poets. His seven previous books of poetry are all still in print. His poetry has been performed by The Royal Shakespeare Company on both sides of the Atlantic and has enjoyed wide success on the radio, in scores of English language newspapers and on countless internet sites. Sky Arts recently aired an hour-long television documentary focused on his poetry and organisations as diverse as The Royal Marines, the MCC and The National Trust have adopted his poems for their own use. His hugely popular poetry recitals pack theatres across Britain, Ireland and the USA.

As a lover of trees, his lifetime ambition is the planting of a large native forest in the Heart of England. He has homes in England, the USA and St. Vincent and the Grenadines.

For more of his poetry or to watch him performing live visit:
www.felixdennis.com

To view progress on Felix's forest project visit:
www.heartofenglandforest.com

'Life is much too short
To be taken seriously.'

— *Nicholas Bentley*